QUEEN,
JEWEL,
MISTRESS

Ruth Stacey

QUEE

JEW

MISTF

RUTH STACEY

N
EL'
ESS

A HISTORY OF THE QUEENS OF
ENGLAND & GREAT BRITAIN IN VERSE

First published in 2015
by Eyewear Publishing Ltd
74 Leith Mansions, Grantully Road
London W9 1LJ
United Kingdom
Typeset with graphic design by Edwin Smet
Author photograph Lawrence Stacey
Printed in England by TJ International Ltd, Padstow, Cornwall

ISBN 978-1-908998-45-3

*Eyewear wishes to thank Jonathan Wonham for his very generous patronage
of our press; as well as our other patrons and investors who wish to remain
anonymous.*

WWW.EYEWEARPUBLISHING.COM

For Pamela Jayne

Ruth Stacey
studied English & Creative Writing
at Bath Spa University and recently completed
a distinction level MA in Literature: *Politics and Identity* at
Worcester University. Her pamphlet *Fox Boy* was published
by Dancing Girl Press in 2014.
She lives in Worcestershire.

Table of Contents

House of Stuart

Commonwealth of England

House of Stuart

House of Hanover

House of Saxe-Coburg and Gotha

House of Windsor

I wish I could tenderly lift from the dark side of history, voices that are anonymous, slighted – inarticulate.

Susan Howe

I swear, 'tis better to be lowly born,
And range with humble livers in content,
Than to be perk'd up in a glistering grief,
And wear a golden sorrow.

King Henry VIII, Act II Scene III
Shakespeare

Listen

how we have heard
of the might of the kings

listen instead
to the voices of queens
hear them echo   echo

House of Wessex

Judith of Flanders

find my thoughts, foolish fly
return restless, red veils
holy house, heated oils
anointed, Aethelwulf waiting

prayers sung, consecrated
willing womb, worshipping
thrones seated, solid strong
Queen crowned, caught fast

       brutal union, brief barren
       old wolf, weeping wastes
       young wolf, yearns offers
       remain regal, royal wife

wild wind, wails low
Aethelbald tempts, tempts tricks
cursed cruel, fates condemn

            i flee   i flee

Wulfthryth

can you hear me?

      listen through distant lives

white limbed
wrapped in a woolen gown
stitched with waves

peaking and crashing into foam

your ear is a cockle shell
hear me whisper

was I queen?

my eyes were green
like young birch leaves

Ealhswith

       then Alfred was King in that stone castle
and well loved, a famous lord of men
and he in turn gave his people two sons
two princes to lead them in battle
such glory, such sword-scorching
suns burning the eyes of all
and I, his wife and Lady
wear silver and jewels
and sing his praise

crying that no better King has ever lived

Æthelflæd

all are below me like rooks
circling   I am the peak
of the mountain

Ælfflæd

daughters melt from mothers
like salt-tears metal
copper blood

I am liquid
they are
from my body

sons are snatched
once they walk they
practise swordplay

my daughters
lean against
my wet ribs

I absorb them, safe
until their maidenhead
breaks and men claim them

Eadgifu of Kent

look now, my little son
you will make a new kingship
and you will sing new songs
          festive, brilliant with torches

how will you attack you reign
so that it differs from your murdered brother?
be a dragon, be a wolf, be a bear
not a mouse, not a minnow, not a woman

Eadred   I worry
will you have his magnificence?

Ælfgifu of Shaftesbury

I am not a concubine
             I am not

his mother's slack hands
hold onto the title
of Queen

I hate the dog-wolves
under the table that wait
for scraps

the gristle in meat
makes me sick

when I asked him
he said/

/ not a concubine

bury me in the nunnery
I am pure

Æthelflæd of Damerham

two leaves drift down
brushing against each other
so briefly

the gilded mark
upon my breast
gold goblets and plate

> the lion is stabbed
> he dies bloody
> without a whimper

the royal smell lingers
on my skin
all men desire me

Ælfgifu

rather than feast at his coronation
the King wanted to feast
                              on me

the bishops' wrath
when faced with his lustful/

 /feet under covers

lawfully married fingers on/

            /naked tips

toad-wet words slipped from slack tongues

base foulest of falsehoods
my mother was not in our bed

God is my witness/

      / punish them

Ælfthryth

King Edgar strong-arm   sent Æthelwald to report   my beauty
one look   he could not resist ravishing   I was his wife
I waited for my King to come   he had been betrayed   come
come   a messenger heralded   dogs bounding   horses dust
Æthelwald begged me to be a crone   hag   dirt   stoop
I washed my hair   catkins   sunlight   lustre of pearl
my gown slipped   shoulders white   bud-rose blooming
the King shuddered   his eyes weak   at my feet
dawn hunting   Edgar slayed Æthelwald   pig gutted
the blood came flooding forth   red   red   vengence
Edgar crowned me   holy oil   bracelets of gold
too soon death claimed him   hard limbs   hidden clouds
my son must be the next King   he must   he must be King
not the child of his first wife   not Edward   my blood   mine
I gave my servent Edgar's hunting knife   sharp   dog-teeth
I offered wine to the boy   blind   innocent   treachery
the blade cut deep   he wept as he fled   died on his horse
I ruled well   stronger   longer than the murmers of evil
until my son was a man   he was King   he was   my blood

House of Denmark

Ælfgifu of York

And so he came across the ocean
Came across the ship-sinker
Came to find his fortune
Came to find Ælfgifu

Cnut my night-prowler
Moon-howler
Bite my thighs
Kiss my mouth
Wet me

Take your Norman wife
Take her if you must
Take her so she gives you
Hill-strength
None will doubt you
King of the English

I am still your Queen
Ælfgifu knows your secret places
Cnut my night-prowler
Our sons are still mightier
Than her whelps

Emma of Normandy

Æthelred, said I, you should do as I say.
I am wise: God blesses me when I pray.
Our son should be your heir, that is right,
Not Edmund son of your previous night.
He listens whilst entwined we are lay –
My mouth gentle, I know how to fight.
Words triumph: he consents in the night.

Æthelred, you are dead, your words ash.
I feel the pressure of warfare and the lash
Of Edmund's tongue barking at me to flee:
My sons and I go in haste to Normandy.
Yet things erupt like blood from a gash,
Cnut is the new King and he desires me.
I will marry him, if Queen again I shall be.

Brave Cnut, said I, you should do as I say.
I am older and wiser: God listens as I pray.
Our son should be your heir, that is right,
Not the sons of Ælgifu, base born and slight.
He listens whilst entwined we are lay –
My mouth gentle, I know how to fight.
Words triumph: he consents in the night.

House of Wessex

Edith Godwine

Anything I can do, here on this earth
To earn your love, O great King, anything
More than I have done I will do

Summon me
I will come as I came
    Once before on our wedding night
  Only for you to not taste the fruit

Take me, my King, my Edward
I am Godwin's daughter, a deserving Queen
With none of the niggardly ways of women
I will not be imperious, my tongue is not vicious
Yet I speak commandingly

Let me now cajole you softly

Come to me
    Give me a child, glorious and great
To continue our royal house

You are as remote as a cloud
Cold depths of the sea
Between us your brother's eyes, put out
On my father's orders

I did not steal the light from Alfred Ætheling
    Godwin has an ambitious air
I am just his breath blown and now belonging
To you, O great King

There must be a child
I demand you come to me   come to me

Ealdgyth of Mercia

I long for Gruffydd, he longs for me
Hearest thou his voice? It is in the wind
Wailing, we will be joined again

A dark day, sun low in misery
Battle swords sharpened, Harold leading
Longing to slay my Gruffydd, I hoping

Message of blood, limbs hacked
Weeping, wretched
Harold taking me in his tent

Stiffened, unmoving, a dead tree
Bloody babe born of sadness
Offers no comfort

Gruffydd dead in the lee shadow
The mountain takes him in
He turns to slate and shale

Queen in rain weather, light refusing
To hold me in its brightness
Harold looks one way, I another

Battle cries, swarm from the north
They come from across the sea
It forms a circle, death

Arrows – Harold hewn to pieces
His swan mistress inspects the corpses
Her tears fall on his birthmarks

Gruffydd, Gruffydd waiting for thee
Has left me light as a leaf whipped
By the west wind to the sea

House of Normandy

Matilda of Flanders

My Matilda, said he, I will be the King,
To England I go and of battle you will sing
So I seek your blessing and wise reasoning.
My ships: I can more than seven hundred take,
I will fight the Saxons and their backs break,
Your face is fairer than my tongue can sing,
Matilda, speak, so I may begin my journeying.

I love you well sir, said I to my Lord,
Take all your might and break the English hordes,
Show no mercy and offer no accord.
Any in your way, cut down till they lie dead
And lift the golden crown to your rightful head.
My counsel: go in haste and make me a Queen,
Fight the bloodiest battle there has ever been,
Maim until you satisfy your vengeful spleen.

To prepare you my Lord and all men around,
A feast of venison and flagons will be found,
Bid them drink and wear a courageous mien,
And then go in speed to make Matilda the Queen.

Matilda of Scotland

The royal blood of Wessex: red like a rosehip
beneath my white skin, an apple just out of reach
at the top of the tree, a deer hunted by lustful dogs.
Nuns wrapped me in candlelight and meek prayers.

Stamping on their veils, still they piously guarded
the treasure from the covetous until I was claimed.
Henry needed my veins; Saxon and Norman joined
as one body, his unstable throne buttressed.

I shed my Saxon name like an adder skin: Edith.
His mother's name fit me like a velvet mantle: Matilda.

Adelicia of Louvain

Like a gnarled tree,
He enveloped me.

A grey pelt of hair,
I am led to his lair.

Clasped by his side,
He will never let me hide.

Ripping me some tender meat,
A lick of something sweet.

I have no other Queenly tasks;
Conceive is all he asks.

Constant grief in his sigh,
Why did his son have to die?

To survive birth and infancy,
Only to drown a man at sea.

The King seeks to replace that life,
Inside the belly of his new wife.

All around his bastards wait,
Hoping for a lucky fate.

My child would be the lawful King,
How I quietly pray for him.

Empress Matilda

My womb, my breasts: discount these.
Am I not my father's child?
Am I not the rightful heir?
Answer me, you fools.

The moon in her cycle
Draws my blood,
Despite gore on your swords
This frightens you.

I am the daughter of a wise King,
Three lusty sons grew in my body.
Yet I am weak and petal soft
With none of their attributes?

Cannot one man in the room
See the idiocy of this notion?
I am fit to rule.
I am my father's child.

I should not speak this way?
You will teach me how to behave?
You should bow down on bended knee
When you approach your Queen.

House of Blois

Matilda of Boulogne

A cell, four walls enclosing,
Silence, contemplation.

Voluntarily walled in, praying,
Helmid, female hermit.

Spending her life, petitioning
The Lord, for our sakes.

Duty to God, life journeying,
One hope, pious pathway.

Duty to Stephen, rightful King,
Royal wife, gentle Queen.

A bed, four posts enclosing,
Devoted, tender sleep.

Devout monarch, meekly obeying,
Will enable, God's blessing.

House of Anjou

Eleanor of Aquitaine

I am a prisoner, alas! To flee
these walls and journey
south; how I long to be free
but Henry fears my truth.

He cannot speak with me,
for I will tell him he is cursed
and he will believe me –
priest blood will kill him.

O cruel jailor! False knight,
plotter and divider!
I long to strip his armour
and crack his shield in two.

And yet, there was a time
he fell from his horse; I ran
as if I would die if he were dead –
the minstrel sings of constant

hearts: I say love and hate
are stalwart bedfellows.

Berengaria of Navarre

Why will a caged thrush still sing?
What does each day bring but an enslaved life?
The sky and cloud wisps in her sight
Yet no flight, no feathers taut with breeze.
Why does the bird not put its fragile head
Beneath its wing and die from grief?

Why does a Lady yearn for her King?
What does each day bring but dust?
He burns with Crusading fire,
Ordered by a higher power.
Less important: one sad wife
Who waits to walk on English soil.

> He tells me apple blossoms
> Are the sweetest English flower,
> But says he does not care for them
> Nor for any bloom or bower.

Isabella of Angoulême

He took me in my twelfth year.
Now he is dead and my boy
will be King; I crown him
in my chamber, at my feet,
with my own golden circlet.
Ha! The crown jewels are lost
in the Wash, lost like John's
heart beat, lost like a young
girl's love of hiding in peace.
I am hated by the people.
Ha! Their hate is feeble.
It must be nurtured, kept
like a plum stone in the palm;
hidden behind long hair
a bear's stare, a bear's maw.

House of Plantagenet

Eleanor of Provence

In the dawn I am a swallow,
Migrating north to breed.
Lady Queen of a frosted realm.

At noon I am a robin,
Fiercely defending my children.
Heart-blood clouding the mind.

In the twilight I am a magpie,
Gathering wealth efficiently;
Extracting each gram of queens-gold.

At dusk I am a nightingale,
With the sweetest voice caressing
The King's ear: his little night bird.

At midnight I am an owl.
Long thoughts in long hours,
Wise plans to promote my own kin.

In the death hour birds will exist
More substantial than I, the tone
Of my voice shall be lost in the sky.

Eleanor of Castile

To be with him at any cost
because I am small
and he is vast.

I long for indigo shadows
beneath trees,
wet grass,
freezing water from the ground.

Shimmer of heat distorting
the rocks on the horizon
into a cross.
All eyes swing to it.

Undulating dull-orange sands.
Dust beneath my fingernails.

In every crease, fabric, veiled mouth
dry – we do not speak.

The noise of tents
creaking, the sudden flap.
When a breeze touches my cheek
I turn to it like a lover.

Holy War, men are dying,
as I bring forth my female child.

The heat evaporates my screams,
my blood dries quickly.

Her eyes are the blue
I was seeking.

Margaret of France

Tallest of tall trees in a field of thin grasses,
Strong shield aloft and his sword arm solid,
Prince portrayed in purest gold cloth,
Helm he holds up and he hastily kisses,
Takes his leave from the lords and ladies.
Up on his horse to unleash war on the Scots.

The great tree falling, the canopy unfilled.
Solace of all sorrow when summer cools,
Cold cheer of comfortless mead and meats,
Leaves fall and flutter, misfortunes gather.
Observe from the abbey, the acorn and axe,
The old oak rots, overwhelmed by old days.

Isabella of France

I will not take my knife
and grind it on a stone.

I will not plunge it through your flesh
and into bone

I will not pluck your
eyes from each false socket or slash

your untrue heart
watching greedily as

the maggot soul parts from the body
or your blood drips

true, death comes to us all
yet there are different ways

to become dead
and my way, you will suffer

I will not hone the metal
until it sharply gleams

but hold it in a fierce flame
burning red then white then you scream

Philippa of Hainault

As with all potential queens I was inspected
Years before when I was just a girl,
And to make me laugh the King recounted
The list of all my features, thus:

Not uncomely hair, betwixt blue-black and brown.
Head is clean-shaped.
Face is narrow and slender
(Like a fox, he whispered).
Eyes are blackish-brown and deep.
Nose is fairly smooth
Save that it is somewhat broad and flattened,
Yet it is no snub-nose
(He kissed me on the tip).
Mouth fairly wide
Lips somewhat full
Especially the lower lip.
(Here the kisses distracted from the telling).
Teeth, which have fallen and grown again are white enough.
The lower teeth project a little beyond the upper,
Yet this is but little seen.
Ears and chin are comely enough.
(He chuckled as he stroked me soft).
Shoulders and lower limbs are reasonably well shapen;
All limbs are well set and unmaimed;
She is of brown skin all over like her father.
(The King investigated this claim thoroughly).

I asked him sweet why he did choose me,
As all my sisters were potential brides;
Was it my education, elegance or beauty?

'My spies all said you were the plumpest.
For making sons, you are the best.'
He laughed and grabbed my thighs.

I prayed as he clasped my hips
On our wedding night,
That very soon he would be right.

Anne of Bohemia

God, if you desire your subjects to be
blessed with a child that is pure and wise,
we shall be meek and pray constantly
and we will undertake any enterprise.
If you may show us in a vision our task,
I swear we can undertake all you ask.

God, we believe in staying chaste and true.
A King and Queen should be far above
other mortals who weakly venerate you.
Richard and I are suffused with love
but do not basely foul it with animal lust:
coupling is far beyond our disgust.

God, we rule this barbaric England
in the style of the Confessor's peace.
We appeal to you, we do not demand;
please make all civil uprisings cease
and bless our celibate bodies,
prove our sainthood to all: hear our pleas.

Isabella of Valois

Ding, dong, bell
  Richard's gone to hell.
Who put him in?
  His own living kin.
Who threw you out?
  Bolingbroke, no doubt.

What kind of man could be so mean
To try to force the little Queen,
Who ne'er did him any harm
But tried to please all with her charm.

Ding, dong, bell
  Hear the Queen yell.
Don't thee want to marry
  The new heir Harry?
I will not, no not I,
  I would rather die.

What kind of man could be so mean
To try to force the little Queen,
Who ne'er did him any harm
But tried to please all with her charm.

Ding, dong, bell
  In France I dwell.
Who threw you out?
  Bolingbroke, no doubt.
I do wish Richard had been stronger,
  And I his Queen a little longer.

House of Lancaster

Joan of Navarre

Witchcraft, that insidious lie!
Used by men to make women die.
It ruins the rich or the poor and mean
from a lowly serf to a noble Queen.
Despite protective wealth and power
sick fear can strike at any hour.

The Prince of Wales I treated well,
despite in mischief he did dwell.
But on his father's death he cursed me,
coveting my dower he befouled me.
His eyes were on the French and war,
to recoup his costly win at Agincourt.

I was accused of treasoning;
conjuring spells to destroy the King.
I had no defense; a lie is solid proof,
stone in the mouths of men: the truth —
they would kill me if I spoke,
to obey was my only hope.

The young King felt remorse and sent
cloth and gifts but it little meant:
I felt joy at his early death,
to be the one alive and left,
enjoying warm sun on my cheek,
to still feel grief and laugh and speak.

Catherine of Valois

A widow at twenty-one,
Handsome Harry dead and gone,
Barely married or enjoyed,
Now left in a Queenly void.
My fecundity a flaw,
Not by reason but by law.
I need my royal son's consent,
'Tis a ploy used to prevent,
Remarry and a forfeit:
Land revoked if I commit.
Until his majority,
A prisoner of law I be,
Caught in a web of tricks,
My sweet King is only six.
If I wait 'til he say 'Yay,'
It will be my dying day.
Instead I'll decide my fate
And handpick a worthy mate.
A poor servant I'll choose,
A man with no lands to lose.
I see him from my window,
Stripped about to swim below.
The water wets his beauty
Pale and tall like a birch tree.
I disguise well as a maid,
My Queenly ways blend and fade.
I join the servants and swim,
Sun blinding, I flow to him,
Hands find a grip, we embrace,
And gently he bites my face.

He tricked by my low guises
Fierce with desire: soft steam rises.
Poor man embracing treason,
Fear for him returns reason.
I pull away and escape,
Return to my Queenly shape.
Serving dinner long he stares
At what my bruised cheek declares,
I'm his woman in that hall –
In his eyes my raiment falls.

Marguerite of Anjou

By the Quene

By mine own hand,
An explanation of tragic circumstances
That hath befallen this land.

Henry, what else could I do? Tell me.
I had no choice, for our son's future throne,
Than to lead the Lancastrian army.

My Henry, you are a weakly pious man.
You made me walk with York to the Abbey,
We bled hate as we paraded that sham.

You should have been a monk not a King,
Benevolent man, you did not perceive
What your prayers would bring.

I was forced to make decisions and rule,
York gathered his forces and civil war loomed,
Men called you a feeble-minded fool.

Our newborn son before you, there was no flicker.
Yet I tended you, wiped you and fed you.
Ominous fear as you became sicker.

Now our brave son is dead, executed for our cause.
Hope is lost; my heart is a dead yew tree.
Despite all this I am still yours.

I know not if these words will reach you,
Now is the time for your prayers.
I fear for your safety,

Marguerite

House of York

Elizabeth Wydeville

I remember a beautiful white woman kneeling beneath a tree,
a handsome, eager man helping her to rise,
love thick like sticky sap betwixt the two:
their eyes glistening, beholding themselves in a mirror.

A cultured, elegant Queen anointed in holy oils and pageantry,
a merry King removing her crown and haughty expressions.
People cheering the celebrations of each new child,
wine and ale soaking the murmurs of the enemy.

A frightened Queen with her children fleeing to Sanctuary,
a bloated, frivolous King dead: her heart in his stone fingers.
The wolves circling the Abbey-Gloucester betraying her,
comforting frightened eyes, voices lost in cloisters.

A naïve Queen listening to the Archbishop swear on his soul,
the new King only needed his brother's cheerful fellowship.
In the star chamber the Queen believing the oath of surety,
noticed how her youngest son's hair smelt of rosemary.

A mother, not a Queen, kissing her child all over his beloved face:
'tell the King, your brother how I love thee both, how you look
exactly like your Father and I will kiss you now for God knoweth
when we shall kiss again, farewell, farewell,' she swooned.

A pale Queen waiting, praying that her trust would no be in vain.
A dreaming King and his small brother snuffed out like lamps.
The news was wept into her ear, her soul stiffened like sealing wax.
What grief – a mother can only resurrect life by remembering it again:

I remember a beautiful white woman kneeling beneath a tree,
a handsome, eager man helping her to rise,
love thick like sticky sap betwixt the two:
their eyes glistening, beholding themselves in a mirror.

Anne Neville

A ball tossed between men's hands,
Quickly held and then thrown as if too hot.

A slender reed to be woven,
Thatched into whichever family were rising.

A red rose, a white rose
And between them: one thin girl.

The enemy now becomes our ally,
Marriage and I am now a princess.

He wound my hair around my limbs,
Binding me with long lengths,

So I lay utterly still as he entered me
In those owl-grey, fleeting nights.

Then brutal men decided battles
Must be fought and death must win.

My prince cut down like a sapling,
The tide ebbs and flows to York.

Gloucester may well be the man,
Who murdered my red Prince,

Such a union is odious and desperate,
But it is the only clear pathway.

Protection and ambition combine,
Loveless, yet a throne may satisfy.

I lie utterly still in our marriage bed,
He has my body but not my head.

House of Tudor

Elizabeth of York

In dark seclusion my maids and I sit waiting for the birth of this child.
The windows are hung with tapestries; the floor is thick with rushes
and still a bitter wind creeps in and feels my swollen body.
The child stirs inside me but I am already turning to dust. I crumble
into long silences, only the rain speaks to me, be patient: soon.

My thoughts are pinpricks of hawthorn, a poisonous grief spreads;
I see two dead boys, two pale rose buds withering. My small girl,
her perfectly formed lids closed over her green eyes, I reach for her
but wake to nothing. Three children laugh and breathe, three buried
in the worm filled soil, one flaps like a tired fish inside me.

My body is bruised by the memory of a baby asleep on my lap,
his lamb breath on my neck; my skin remembers him. It was snowing
as I gave birth, a winter night with the wind buffeting the walls
yet all the heat of the world was captured in the skin of my newborn,
his small cry encircled my heart.

My fingertips still burn from his fever; they peeled back my hands
from his stiffened body and buried my Edmund in the Abbey.
Grief is a crow that will not roost: Arthur too is dead, the palace
is a pile of bones, all our hopes but one are bones, so I sit heavy
with a child I have foreseen will be the death of me.

I am not frightened. The unborn child moves to please us,
I try to cherish it but I am made of smoke. My young brothers
come to me in my dreams and tell me to be patient: soon.
No flowers last in this darkness, all the white roses wilt.
I gather up the petals and place them on my tongue.

Katherine of Aragon

My most dear lord, King and husband,
The hour of my death now drawing on
The tender love I owe you forces me
To plead that you safeguard your soul.
You should think of heavenly matters
Rather than the pampering of your body.

Soon you shall not see the brightness
Of this world nor move your tongue
To pray and your limbs will melt
Away in sweat from the pain and agony
Of death – then deign to think of me above
With the company of angels where

You cannot pass, my love.

Anne Boleyn

Deer do not tremble, I know this.
My bone and sinew twisted into fallow
slenderness and the tibia twig thin.

Four rods finished with a cloven
hoof planted on rotting leaf mould:
gloomy weight of the gold altar.

The poet's words are wind-blown apples.
Plucked lute strings vibrate to silence
as I watch Caesar with my velvet eyes,

long ears poised to absorb
the rush of animal clamour that is hushed
in the shells of human skulls.

Despite the blood threat of power
my doe body would not spring away –
no flick of spotted fur into shadow.

Jane Seymour

The sea, the sea,
it is here in the room
washing over me;
can you not hear it?
There is a wolf in my bed
gnawing at my stomach,
it is agony, agony.

Where is my son?
Bring him to me,
I order you.
I am the Queen.
Where is the King?

Listen:
mocking laughter.
Can you not hear it?
Her voice, so sweet,
so charming.
singing like a nightingale,
but she was a night crow.

It was right to spy,
supplant the whore.
God has rewarded
my goodness
with a son.

Why do you all stare?
Make this pain stop

I beg you.
It is agony, agony.
The bed is full of blood
like a crimson sea –
the wolf has slunk away.

Anne of Cleves

The dour painter made me stand and face him.
He said, 'Sit and do not move, not slightly.'
To me the light appeared a little dim,
But I cast my dark eyes down politely.

He snapped and barked at me to look ahead
And held my eyes with his intriguing pair.
Lifting the brush to show the shade of red,
Hair and pigment suffused his probing stare.

'Mistress,' he said, 'you are kind and comely,
I see the beauty of your inner soul:
Gentle with an obvious purity,
I shall paint your skin as soft as a foal.'

Did we care if the King agreed with this?
No, we just melted into oil paint bliss.

Catharine Howard

And will thou leave me thus? Naked as a calf
that has been fattened for the table. Stay
here in my bedchamber – stay and play.
Say yes! For the sake of love, stay!
Would you leave your little white calf?

Tom, will thou leave so soon? The door
is guarded against the slumbering King.
Who cares what the morn may bring,
say yes! Say yes to love; come sing!
Tom, say you will not open that door.

I must stay; stay and satisfy the royal bull.
He gives me gold to bruise my thighs;
jewels – I kiss and fawn and lie,
his bulk so great I long to die.
My family fed me to the royal bull.

And will thou leave me thus? Unsatisfied,
when I long for you: smooth skin,
white teeth – gasping the words of a hymn
as I become liquid and forget the King.
All thoughts whiten…I am satisfied.

Katherine Parr

It is the rope I envisage behind my peaceful countenance,
contracting in decreasing turns, tightening and the pain
echoed by the smoulder that follows from the faggots
heaped about her feet as I dance in my brocade skirts;
a heavy gift from my most noble King and husband.
He watches me and his eyes are acrid and suffocating.

Panic is like a kind of burning, it engulfs me entirely
until I blaze like a willow tree struck by lightning.
My bodice is sodden with sweat as I step and curtsy,
spin to the left in time to the music and step towards
the scaffold, the sharp metal edge of axe and enemies
watch as I retire to my rooms: all I can do is scream.

Jane Grey

Last words written by Queen Jane:

Put only your trust in God –
I did not desire to be Queen.

Protestant rule is righteous,
but not based on a falsehood.
Ambitious relatives used me.
Edward, in his death duress
tired to stitch a new history:
this misshapen royal bloodline.
I did not desire to be Queen.
My own flesh cruelly beat
each limb until I obeyed them.
O Crown! A vale of misery
weighs upon my humble brow.
I aspire now to that place:
heavenly throne of joy with
Christ our true saviour and King.

I did not desire to be Queen –
put only your trust in God.

Mary I

I pray. The words constantly accompany me.
God listens. I place my hands upon my child.
See you not my belly, large with my son?
A lusty son for a Catholic England.
On the edge of my mind I wait for the bawl
of my babe. Listen – the screams from Smithfield
gush into any silence so I allow no silence.
Why were the heretics not gagged?
The faggots were blown out by the wind.
Philip has gone to Flanders, gone, gone.
Come back my love, it was not I who refused
to have you crowned, come back.
See you not my belly, large with your son?
My golden father cast me out of his orbit.
I am a good Catholic, I bring the Holy Church
back to this land of heretics, O my dead Mother –
why is the summer so blistering?
The crops fail and the sun scorches the soil.
The day of my child's birth passes, weeks
slip by and all eyes are piteous.
There must be a baby, there must.
God loves me. Philip will love me.
The baby will love me. I pray.
Love me. Love me. Love me.

Elizabeth I

Woman was made to serve and obey man,
Man must obey God. Wife: man can command.

A natural order, God's ordained plan;
A woman must bow down to her husband.

> *England needs an heir so I must marry*
> *But yet I prevaricate and tarry.*

A Queen when she weds is suddenly less,
The elevated bridegroom now soars high.

The prize: Kingship and a Queen to undress,
To win this all men would flatter and lie.

> *Robert Dudley calls me and I long to go,*
> *For I am soft and made of melting snow.*

Once wedded the Queen is precarious,
At the mercy and caprice of the King.

Childbirth deadly, bloody and dangerous,
The dire consequence of mortal loving.

> *A virgin Queen I am and will remain.*
> *No man commands: I rule, ever the same.*

House of Stuart

Anne of Denmark

Queen across the sea and storm,
Saved from dying in the deep.
Enthroned to watch you perform,
The role of wife, mine to keep.

    Your Queen entreats on thy good will,
      I am your jewel and mistress still.

The court is a flock of birds,
Cawing voices seek out gold.
Gallants win favours with words,
The handsome tighten their hold.

    Your wife entreats on thy good will,
      I am your jewel and mistress still.

James the oil did mark me,
Our hearts are one, be not cruel.
Anointed, it doth bind thee,
I beg, let not thy fools rule.

    Your Anne entreats on thy good will,
      I am your jewel and mistress still.

Henrietta Maria of France

May the years and long hours
Garland my dear love with flowers.

May the angels brightly sing
And help me in remembering.

His Queen, still mortal, waits to die
And join her King in peace on high.

Charles the sovereign of my spring.
No flowers bloom for I, less him.

Prince in Heaven sweeter yet,
Than any earthly son I did beget.

All others pale if I compare,
This perfect love: our flawless pair.

Our life was one of growing silence,
As we met with less allegiance.

We turned deaf ears and folding,
Petals overlapping, holding.

Until we only spoke together,
Voices fluffed like chicken feathers.

One day my fading sun will set,
And then this Queen will be well met.

Commonwealth of England

Elizabeth Cromwell

Solemn, sober and modest,
blessed are ye that weep now,
for ye shall laugh.

Controlled emotions,
result in meek and Godly folk.
Rewarded hereafter.

Skin free from paint,
breasts swathed in humble cloth.
Righteous beauty.

Against the bedpost,
he makes me breathless,
all laughter silenced.

But when we finish he
laughs by my ear and calls me
his Queen.

House of Stuart

Catherine of Braganza

How do I tolerate each eager mistress?
How can I share the man I long to kiss?
Because they can never be his holy wife,
Anointed in heaven and joined for life.

A wench can act the lady and ascend,
A good actress swathed in silks can blend
Into the court of noble creatures
Using her wit and comely features.

So Charles will send for silly Nell,
Her laugh is like a silver chiming bell.
The court is always gay and witty
And she the quickest wit and pretty.

Wilmot laughs and calls her just a jester,
He is right, that clever rake Rochester.
He and I both know Charles loves a wit,
The cutting quickness of a clever quip.

The King loves most those who do amuse,
For the duller mistresses it doth confuse,
Why I sit and smile at Nelly's capering:
I will do anything to please my King.

He'll press my hand and kiss it oft,
And whilst he treats me thus soft,
His eyes will darken and he tells me
He loves no other like his Queen Bee.

Mary of Modena

They taught me that
A Queen must be dutiful,
Love her husband;
Be fruitful.

They did not mention:
The pitted skin of an old man,
Religious strife,
A warming pan.

Lies, slander, plots,
Take my King to his tomb.
Our son is the true heir
Of *my* womb.

My son is not a changeling –
Every pamphlet is a lie.
Witnesses saw my blood,
Heard his first cry.

Politics forces us to flee:
I am Queen across the water.
My boy eager for his crown,
I fear his slaughter.

Exiled from his throne,
James will often curse and weep:
But I pray each hour, each day,
His royal life to keep.

Mary II

Tremulous thoughts recall
my marriage night:
faced with a groom
misshapen as ancient
branches of ivy and as cold
as the shadow that creeps
at the bottom of a well.
I shuddered and longed to flee.

Duty in the bedchamber;
the union my family desired.
Efficient hands unwrapped
my tear-sodden gown, consolation
in the eyes of my women.
Candles blazed and voices hooted
ribald jokes, merriment
from jostling courtiers.

Then the doors were shut,
the silence boomed.
Gloom increasing as William
walked about the room
and blew the candles out.
Gilded token,
from my father's fingers
into his clammy hand.

Yet unhappiness can be
controlled with deference.
Love *can* take root

in the garden of duty.
His approval is my
reward in this brief life.
William is my master:
he is pleased with me.

Anne

Beginning

Sarah's striking looks her inner beauty show,
An iced soul that makes her white skin glow.
Strong though her mind, gentle her hands,
Fevered my brow, which my love fans.
Outside a whirling storm of statecraft –
Inside Mrs. Morley and Mrs. Freeman laugh.
Each night to our husbands we retire, content,
These fine men to whom we are merely lent.
Our days: we comb my hair and discuss each fig
Of juicy gossip about some dull Tory or Whig.
I tremble as my stern Sarah above me reigns,
Her harsh words excite and ignite my veins.

Middle

Mrs. Freeman's babies live, each birthday pass,
My body swells yet my infants die, alas.
The hope is granite; I bend beneath the weight
Of each shattered hope, this tragic fate.
My dear George laments the cruelty of life
In the fond bosom of I, his faithful wife.
Thus, as I comfort him and gain strength of heart,
Sarah Churchill snaps – her tempers start.
A veil is lifted: she despises Mrs. Morley.
Her love was an act, I am wounded sorely.
I banish her and refuse to hear her plea;
She no longer holds the royal key.

End

In safe, dull repose my last few hours to spend,
I am not fearful, nor impatient of their end.
My thoughts linger on she whom I dare not recall,
How her strident voice held my heart in thrall:
One impatient glance, a tap on my skin with a fan,
Her eyes fierce like a lion, I lay down like a lamb.

House of Hanover

Sophia Dorothea of Celle

To fall in love and choose your own mate,
Would enable a contented happy fate.

Marriage is a contract between men of power,
Strengthening alliances through land and dower.

Cousins must marry to keep lands together,
Despite mutual disgust, two are bound forever.

Hatred and contempt form the marriage bed,
Both heartily wishing the other one dead.

Two children conceived, the duty is done,
The mind turns to pleasure, romance and fun.

Falling in love is sucking honey from a spoon,
An explosion of sweetness in a habitual room.

I know my husband is rutting with some maid,
And none care a jot in whose bed he is laid.

So when I am caught in the arms of my lover,
I ask George how he is allowed all those others?

He rages and howls and beats my white skin,
Purple bruises like roses, designed by him.

They hold him back as he tries to rip me apart,
His male dignity screaming yet not his heart.

Thirty years he has kept me locked in a tower,
To show me he holds the keys to power.

I can't kiss my children again in this life,
And I curse the dread day I became his wife.

Caroline of Brandenburg-Ansbach

This is a truthful account of my diligent life,
I was never a subservient Queen or wife.
My husband, whose constant passion is drink,
Lapping rich foods and loath to think:
I am the opposite jewel, a shine to his shade,
Choosing his suit the wisest decision I made.
Rejecting an Emperor and the King of Spain,
I embraced George's body as my new domain.
Wisdom, intelligence, a leader of fashion –
I inspired in people devotion and passion.
Used my deft diplomacy nous to aid policy,
Walpole, my confidant, consulting with me.
Party leaders knew I was the one to woo,
Queen Caroline ruled Britain: this is true.

Charlotte of Mecklenburg-Strelitz

What is madness?
Losing the Colonies

       that vast wilderness,
       impossible to tame

where bears and cougars
pace in mountains

and the people have uncouth
desires to be free.

The head of an elegant
French Queen dressed

       in ribbons and powder,
severed by a guillotine.

The muttering of a King,
talking to his two dead sons

the evil humours form
his living shroud.

Caroline of Brunswick-Wolfenbüttel

He resembles a goose, elegantly stuffed.
Decorated in white velvet and ruffles,
glowing with pearls on each limb,
his wide mouth curling in a grimace.
Disgust, because of me? I disappoint him.

His manners are sublime, so perfect,
yet he reminds me I am his subject.
Blinking as if I lead him to slaughter,
his dry skin skims mine like an insect
balancing on stagnant pond water.

We have done our duty: two cats hissing,
mouths held far apart, never kissing.
He swears he will not touch me again.
O handsome Prince, you are dismissing
me? I vow that I will plague you and remain.

Adelaide of Saxe-Meiningen

Love me, English people with your hearts,
Show sweetly tender loyalty.
Love me when our dearest King departs,
Though there be novel royalty.

Spare a thought for gentle Adelaide,
When the little Queen's bless'd and crown'd,
Recall as you cheer the gold parade,
To oblivion I am bound.

A shadow Queen without King or throne,
Is into the empty ether hurled.
I *am* a Queen in my skin and bone,
So now seem of no use in this world.

Victoria

I am Queen and I shall do my utmost to fulfil
my duty towards my country.

Duty is a slapped mouth, sewn shut with cat-gut.

To my dear, loyal subjects who are assembled to show
their good humour and excessive loyalty.

Apes, hyenas, jackdaws: how they screech and caw.

How proud I felt to be the Queen of such a Nation,
the Crown being placed on my head, so gently.

But such a weight! Monstrous as a beached whale.

It was, I remember, a most beautiful, impressive moment.
My robes draped on the chair beautifully.

White body full of blood, bruises that bleed.

Nothing was done without his loving advice and help,
darling Albert was the other part of me.

Filled with life after life after life after life after life.

The only ray of comfort I get for a moment is in the firm
conviction and certainty

I remember the chloroform. So blissfully empty of voices.

of his nearness, his undying love and of our eternal reunion.
Impatiently I wait and I do my *damn* duty.

House of
Saxe-Coburg and Gotha

Alexandra of Denmark

My dreamscapes form
into vast Russian cities
I have never visited.
When I cannot stand it
a moment longer I wake.
Fears turn to warm milk,
tea, sugar, and their ilk.
Safety in the breakfast tray
…and *it* is not a sin.
For our own sakes
we must not offer them
sanctuary, my dear son
George has explained
it all to me. I understand
the danger of infection
spreading, revolution
arriving in dear England.
It must be protected.
Thoughts must be banished,
like when my darling Eddy
died and I buried my angel.
Pain flourished,
I grew unsteady.
Punished by grief and ready
to lie down and die.
This could not be,
I had to be stronger.
push away sadness
dwell no longer.
Although I confess

I weep in private still,
but things in Russia
will resolve in time,
my sister is fine.
She writes that Nicky
is in his prime,
a handsome Tsar.
Things are as they should be,
things are right as they are.
Dowager Queens should not meddle,
and yes, two sugars in my tea.

House of Windsor

Mary of Teck

Diamonds: suck the light
from the room,
consume it –

suck, suck tiny glaciers,
obliterate the land
of ordinary things.
Shell of sapphires,

refract dullness
into brilliance,
make them
shade their eyes, blink.

Blink, courtiers,
our flesh is far away –
no salt; no salt water.

Elizabeth Bowes Lyon

when bad dreams come like rising fog,
cruel and uncalled for – the melancholy
smell of a city

      burning, the drone and shudder
      of bombers, a storm
overhead: such threats unseen in clouds

why is a soul born to rule and another
man can abdicate without due thought?

a throne that makes a slender throat
tremble or two knees bend before one

the curve of a horse's back in full gallop
can blank all fears and memories

      the shape of the fetlock, the joy
of a mane flowing in the cool air
and the thunder like planes as they pass.

Elizabeth II

In today's correspondence a poetry book
detailing the lives of British Queens –
with a note enclosed and a question:
what does it mean to be a Queen?

I could reply and say –
this precious stone set in a silver sea:
a symbol, like a banner, for mens' love.
But these are not my words.

I could reply and say –
glorying in the glories of my people,
sorrowing with the sorrows of the lowest.
But these are not my words.

I could declare –
that each Queen is tissue paper thin,
translucent but combined, are my flesh.
But I will not solidify my words,

instead I will command my secretary to write,
with many kind thanks for the little book etc,
but to say my thoughts on Queenship
can only be ascertained by my actions.

Notes on the Queens of England & Great Britain

Judith of Flanders (c. 843 – c. 870) was the daughter of Charles the Bald and she was married, aged around fourteen, to Aethelwulf. Charles insisted on her being crowned and accorded this rank, despite it not being customary for kings' wives to be queens in Wessex, rather they were called the king's wife or lady. The marriage only lasted two years. Upon his death, Judith married her stepson Aethelbald.

Wulfthryth was married to Æthelred of Wessex and she was the mother of his sons. Their marriage strengthened the dynastic ties which allied the House of Wessex to that of Mercia.

Ealhswith married Alfred the Great, King of Wessex in 868. After Alfred's death in 899, Ealhswith became a nun. She had five children who survived to adulthood.

Æthelflæd was the eldest daughter of King Alfred the Great of Wessex and Ealhswith. She was the queen of Æthelred and after his death, ruler of Mercia (911 – 918). The Anglo-Saxon Chronicle styles her as the 'Lady of the Mercians' (Myrcna hlæfdige). The dominion of Mercia descended to Ælfwynn, Æthelflæd's heiress but she was compelled to submit to her mother's brother, King Edward the Elder of Wessex. The succession of Edward the Elder finalised the union of the two formerly separate kingdoms of Wessex and Mercia.

Ælfflæd was the second queen of Edward the Elder. She married him c. 901 and became the mother of two sons and six daughters.

Eadgifu of Kent, third queen of Edward the Elder during c. 919 – 924, she became the mother of two sons, Edmund, later King Edmund I, and Eadred, later King Eadred. Eadgifu survived Edward and lived until old age.

Ælfgifu of Shaftesbury was the queen consort of Edmund I and the mother of two Kings. Despite this she was described as the King's concubine (concubina regis). By comparison her mother-in-law, Eadgifu was described as mater regis, only below her sons Edmund and Eadred at court. Ælfgifu died in 944, was buried at Shaftesbury and revered as a saint.

Æthelflæd married Edmund I in 944 following the death of his first wife Ælfgifu, mother of the future Kings Eadwig and Edgar.

Ælfgifu was the consort of King Eadwig of England and she is notorious for distracting the King from his coronation feast by seducing him with her mother. Ælfgifu was most likely slandered by the opposing power faction at court.

Ælfthryth (c. 945 – c. 1001) was the second queen of King Edgar of England. It is said that Edgar sent his subject Æthewald to report on Ælfthryth's beauty. Æthelwald married her himself and sent back a message that she was unsuitable for the King. She was the mother of King Ethelred the Unready and a powerful political figure. She became infamous as an 'evil stepmother' for the alleged murder of her stepson King Edward the Martyr.

Ælfgifu of York (flourished c. 970 – 1002) wife and queen of King Cnut and mother of his two sons, Svein and Harold Harefoot. After his conquest of England in 1016, Cnut married Emma of Normandy, the widow of King Æthelred.

Emma of Normandy (c. 985 – 1052) was the second queen of Aethelred. They had two sons, the future Edward the Confessor and his brother Alfred Ætheling. On Æthelred's death his eldest son from his first marriage, Edmund Ironside became King. Cnut then invaded and took power and married Emma to strengthen his claim. They had a son Harthacnut. Emma and Ælfgifu were both ambitious for their sons and fought hard to ensure their own son was the King. Ælfgifu's son Harold ruled for three years but when he died Harthacnut took the throne. He only ruled for two years and Edward the Confessor became King. He did not give his mother Emma any power and she retired from court.

Edith Godwine (1025-1075) was the daughter of Godwine, Earl of Wessex, one of the most powerful men in England at the time of King Edward's reign. She married King Edward the Confessor of England in 1045. The marriage produced no children; some speculate it was because Edward took a vow of celibacy or perhaps he refused to consummate the marriage because of his antipathy to Edith's family.

Ealdgyth (Edith) of Mercia was supposedly a woman of great beauty. In 1058, Ealdgyth married her first husband Gruffydd ap Llywelyn of Wales. Gruffydd was killed at Snowdonia by the invading army of Harold Godwinson, Earl of Wessex. In 1064 she married Harold, who on 6th January 1066 would be crowned King Harold II of England. Although Ealdgyth was his lawful wife and Queen Consort, Harold Godwinson also had a common-law wife, Edith Swannesha.

Matilda of Flanders (c. 1031 – 1083), queen consort of William the Bastard, Duke of Normandy, was a direct descendent of Alfred the Great. By marrying her William vastly strengthened his claim to the English throne. They had nine children and after her death William became a tyrant; perhaps his grief made him act this way or the lack of her wise council.

Matilda of Scotland (1080-1118) was the first queen of Henry I. She was the daughter of Malcolm of Scotland and her mother was the sister of Edgar the Ætheling and therefore part of the ancient royal family of Wessex. This was important as Henry wanted to make himself more popular with the English people and Matilda represented the old English dynasty. In their children, the Norman and English dynasties would be united. Her daughter was Empress Matilda and although she was unsuccessful in her claim to the throne, through her the bloodline continued with Henry II.

Adelicia of Louvain (1103-1151) was the second queen of Henry I King of England and they married when she was in her late teens and Henry was fifty-three. Despite holding the record for the most illegitimate children of a British monarch, Henry had only one legitimate son, William Adelin, who drowned in 1120 during the White Ship disaster. Henry kept his bride close to him and out of public life, perhaps in the hope she would conceive but no children were born. However after Henry died Adelicia married for a second time and at least seven of her babies survived to adulthood.

Empress Matilda (c. 1102 – 1167), the only daughter and surviving heir of Henry I, was married to Henry V, Holy

Roman Emperor. When he died she was remarried to Geoffrey of Anjou, but retained the title of Empress for the rest of her life. Empress Matilda was the first Queen Regnant but she failed to consolidate her rule and it amounted to only a few months. Her son would rule as Henry II. Historians exclude her from the official list of Monarchs.

Matilda of Boulogne (c. 1105 – 1152) was the queen of Stephen of Blois and she was born in Boulogne, France, the daughter of Eustace III. Matilda was the first cousin of her husband's rival, Empress Matilda. Through her maternal grandmother, Matilda was descended from the pre-Conquest English kings. On the death of Henry I, Stephen rushed to England and was crowned King, beating his rival, the Empress Matilda. In the civil war that followed, known as the Anarchy, Matilda proved to be her husband's strongest supporter.

Eleanor of Aquitaine (c. 1122 – 1204) was the queen of Henry II and one of the most dauntless and brave women of the Middle Ages. Duchess of Aquitaine in her own right she married Louis VII and as Queen of the Franks, she participated in the unsuccessful Second Crusade. Soon after the Crusade was over, Louis VII and Eleanor agreed to dissolve their marriage. Within a few weeks Eleanor married Henry II, Duke of the Normans. He was eleven years younger than her. When Henry ascended the throne of England Eleanor became Queen of the English. Over the next thirteen years, she bore Henry eight children. However, Henry and Eleanor eventually became estranged. She was imprisoned between 1173 and 1189 for supporting her son Henry's revolt against her husband.

Berengaria of Navarre (c. 1165 – 1230), neglected queen of Richard the Lionheart. She never set foot in England as his wife and they remained childless and she was reported to be very distressed when he died. She founded the abbey of L'Épau on the outskirts of Le Mans in 1229 and entered the convent there.

Isabella of Angoulême (c. 1188 – 1246) was the only daughter and heir of Aymer Taillefer, Count of Angoulême, and Alice of Courtenay. She was supposedly a great beauty and King John married her when she was twelve. Isabella was blamed for seducing him from his business although she had little say and no power. They had five children and upon his death Isabella had her eldest son crowned with her own golden circlet to ensure his succession. After this she returned to Angoulême and remarried. She had a further nine children and remarkably all her children survived to adulthood.

Eleanor of Provence (c. 1223 – 1291) was the clever and fashionable queen of King Henry III of England. She was unpopular because of her advancement of her relatives but she was loyal to the King and they had five children. Born in Aix-en-Provence, she was the second eldest daughter of the Count of Provence and Beatrice of Savoy.

Eleanor of Castile (1241 – 1290) the devoted queen of Edward I and the feeling was mutual. The couple were rarely apart and she traveled with him, even on Crusade. She gave birth to her daughter in Acre. A strong woman, she absorbed some of the King's unpopularity, as it was easier to blame a foreign Queen than the King himself. They lost many of their children as infants. When she died Edward built a cross at every point the funeral procession stopped and he mourned her deeply. Even after his second marriage he still attended memorial services for Eleanor.

Margaret of France (c. 1279 – 1318) was the second queen of Edward I and despite being only sixteen and Edward sixty years they had a very successful and happy marriage. They had three children, two sons and a daughter and Edward was (slightly) softened by the love of his young wife and many were saved from his wrath at her intercession.

Isabella of France (1295 – 1358) was queen of Edward II and mistress of Roger Mortimer, with whom she overthrew the King and placed her son on the throne as Edward III. Isabella was educated and elegant. Edward II was a weak King and this weakness enabled revolt and disorder to occur and gave Mortimer the chance to encourage the queen to act as regent. Edward II was murdered. When he came of age Edward III had Mortimer executed and took power back from Isabella.

Philippa of Hainault (1314 – 1369), the wife of Edward III and mother of his fourteen children. Their eldest child was the Black Prince who died before he could become King, and their five remaining sons would set up the different power factions that caused the War of the Roses. It was a happy marriage and she was a popular queen. As a princess, Philippa was examined and a report was sent of her attributes, precise to every detail.

Anne of Bohemia (1366 – 1394) was the first queen of Richard II and the daughter of the Holy Roman Emperor. It was a deeply unpopular marriage. The couple seemed a contented pair, although they had no children and this was a dynastic disaster for Richard II. Anne died of the plague after twelve years of marriage.

Isabella of Valois (1389 – 1409) was the second queen of Richard II and she was the daughter of the King of France, Charles VI. She was only six years old when she married Richard and it is debated that he may have chosen a child bride so he would not have to consummate the marriage and break his vow of celibacy. Richard was deposed and executed by Henry Bolingbroke, who became Henry IV. He tried to marry Isabella to his son, the future Henry V, but she refused and eventually she was returned to France. She married again and had a daughter, Jeanne. Isabella died aged nineteen.

Joan of Navarre (1370 – 1437), second wife and Queen of Henry IV. His first wife gave him many children and died before he became King so his second marriage may have been a love match. There is evidence of an attraction between Joanna and Henry so it was not purely a political move, although Joanna brought him a lot of prestige and helped to secure his newly won throne. Their happiness was sadly cut short by the King's illness, probably leprosy. The new King, Henry V, had a comfortable relationship with his stepmother but his desire for money to fund his warmongering led to a charge of witchcraft.

Catherine of Valois (1401 – 1437) was the younger sister of Isabella of Valois. She married Henry V and gave birth to his son, Henry VI but his father never met him, dying on a French battlefield instead. Catherine was only twenty and caused concern to the young King's protector; fearful of some ambitious Lord marrying her he passed laws that would confiscate the land of any man that did so. Catherine circumnavigated this law by marrying a penniless but handsome Welsh servant, Owen Tudor. Their grandson would eventually rule as Henry Tudor.

Marguerite of Anjou (1430 – 1482) was the Lancastrian (red rose) queen during the wars known as the Wars of the Roses. Due to Henry's frequent bouts of insanity, Marguerite ruled the kingdom in her husband's place. She was a proud woman and determined to secure the throne for her son, Edward of Westminster. Henry VI was a deeply unsuitable King, and was more interested in religion. For some time, whilst Henry VI was a prisoner, Margaret lived in exile in France with her son Edward. The civil war was bloody and despite wins and losses on both sides, eventually Marguerite was defeated and her only son dead on the battlefield.

Elizabeth Wydeville (1437 – 1492) was supposedly very beautiful which caught the King's attention. She was definitely a widow from Grafton Regis with two young sons. Edward IV married her despite the fact she had no lands or wealth and their children included Elizabeth of York and their sons Edward and Richard, the 'princes in the tower'. When Edward IV died, his brother Richard, Duke of Gloucester, took the throne and imprisoned the heir Edward V. The princes died in the tower, though there is no firm evidence to say who murdered them.

Anne Neville (1456 – 1485) was the daughter of Warwick, the Kingmaker. Her father changed sides during the War of the Roses and she was married to Edward of Westminster. She then became Princess of Wales but her young husband was soon slain and she was a wealthy heiress without any protection. She married Richard, Duke of Gloucester. They were crowned when Richard seized the throne but their reign was brief. Their son died and Anne died soon after. Richard did not have time to marry and get a new heir; he died on Bosworth Field and the crown went to Henry Tudor.

Elizabeth of York (1466 – 1503), eldest child of Edward IV, she was betrothed to the Lancastrian claim to the throne, Henry Tudor. He defeated Richard III in battle and married Elizabeth to secure his throne and join the white and red roses together in the Tudor dynasty. Elizabeth was a peaceful, obedient wife who gave birth to seven children. Her namesake died aged three and Edmund at eighteen months. Shortly after their heir, Arthur, died of a fever and caused terrible grief to his parents and fear as they only had one male heir left, the future Henry VIII. Elizabeth is famous for comforting Henry with the words, 'God is where he was and we are both young enough.' She did indeed become pregnant again but died in childbirth aged thirty-seven. The hoped for spare, a girl called Katherine, also died with her mother.

Katherine of Aragon (1485 – 1536) was the first wife of Henry VIII. A pious princess from Spain, she first married his older brother Arthur but when he died she was married to Henry. Unfortunately, their first son died after a month of celebrations and only one baby, Mary, survived to adulthood. Henry desired a male heir and fell in love with Anne Boleyn. The question of 'if' Katherine consummated her marriage with Arthur formed the basis of the divorce, yet she vowed she was a virgin when she married Henry. She remained regal and loyal despite Henry's treatment of her.

Anne Boleyn (c. 1507 – 1536) was the second wife of Henry VIII and the probable muse of the poet Thomas Wyatt. He transformed Anne into a hind for his poem *Whoso List to Hunt*. She used her wit and intelligence to negotiate a marriage with Henry. She was the first queen to be crowned with Edward the Confessor's crown. When she gave birth to the future Elizabeth I and then subsequently miscarried a male child she lost favour with the King. She may also have opposed the dissolution of the monasteries and therefore Thomas Cromwell. He invented a charge of treason and she was executed by having her head cut off with a sword.

Jane Seymour (1508 – 1537), Henry's third queen, was a pale and prim maid of honour and Henry married her with indecent haste after Anne's execution. She died after giving birth to the longed for male child, the future Edward VI, and earned Henry's devotion. He later included her in dynastic portraits despite having new wives. When he died, Henry was buried beside her.

Anne of Cleves (1515 – 1557), fourth wife of Henry and painted by Holbein. She was chosen for this attractive portrait and her Protestant faith. Upon meeting her Henry felt no attraction for her and she was quickly divorced and lived comfortably as the 'King's Sister'.

Catharine Howard (1523 – 1542) was Henry's fifth Queen and Anne Boleyn's cousin. A poor member of the powerful Howard family and niece of the Duke of Northumberland, she was advanced to bring the Catholic family back in favour. A very attractive and young girl, she was promiscuous before marriage and continued to be so after. The enemies of the Howard faction soon discovered the affair with Thomas Culpeper and Catherine was condemned without a trial. Before her execution she practiced placing her head on the block so she would not stumble.

Katherine Parr (1512 – 1548) was the sixth wife of Henry VIII. She was twice widowed and a clever, educated woman. Henry chose her and she had no option but to marry him. She was a mother figure to his motherless children and managed to survive plots to remove her. Her friend, Anne Askew, was burnt for her religious beliefs. On Henry's death she married Thomas Seymour for love but died giving birth to her only child, a little girl who died aged about two.

Jane Grey (1536 – 1554), the daughter of Frances Brandon and a member of the blood royal through her grandmother Mary Tudor, younger sister of Henry VIII. Raised as a strict Lutheran and companion of Edward VI, she was seen as an alternative to the Catholic Mary. Edward named her his heir, a move that was not legal and Jane was married to Guilford Dudley. The Dudley family was insistent on having Guilford crowned King. Jane resolutely refused and within nine days it was all over. Mary was welcomed by the populace and crowned as Mary I. Jane was imprisoned and both she and Guilford were subsequently beheaded.

Mary I (1516 – 1558) was the daughter of Katherine of Aragon and Henry VIII. When her brother Edward died and she became queen, Mary put a lot of effort in to bringing England back to the Catholic faith. This involved burning Protestant heretics and earned her the moniker of 'Bloody Mary'. Despite this crusading mission she desperately wanted to be married and have a child. She chose Philip of Spain and the Catholic monarch brought a wave of unpopular feeling towards Mary. She suffered a phantom pregnancy and Philip left her to go abroad and govern his continental lands.

Elizabeth I (1533 – 1603) was the only child of Anne Boleyn and Henry VIII. She inherited his red hair and royal temper and her mother's black eyes and allure. She was a master of statecraft, spoke six languages and was incredibly wily. She chose not to marry but instead elevated herself above her male courtiers as the Virgin queen of myth. She had a long friendship and affection for Robert Dudley, one of her married courtiers.

Anne of Denmark (1574 – 1619) was the blonde queen of James I of England. On her way to Scotland her ship was forced back to the coast of Norway due to bad weather and James sailed with his retinue to fetch her. The marriage was romantic and successful at first. In time they drifted apart but they retained some affection for each other and James was heartbroken when she died. Anne was a patron of the arts and had seven children. Three survived to adulthood, including the future Charles I.

Henrietta Maria of France (1609 – 1669), queen of Charles I and a staunch Catholic. Their marriage was unsuccessful at first but they eventually fell in love. They celebrated courtly love and etiquette and had a number of children who survived including Charles II and James II. She was deeply unpopular due to her Catholic faith.

Elizabeth Cromwell (1598 – 1665) was the wife of the Lord Protector, Oliver Cromwell. This poem represents the *Interregnum*.

Catherine of Braganza (1638 – 1705) was the queen of the womanising rake King Charles II and she had to put up with his many mistresses. She was a plain woman and unpopular due to being a Catholic. Unfortunately they remained childless, which was a bitter blow as Charles had many illegitimate children. However, Charles was very kind to her and treated her with absolute respect and insisted his mistresses did as well. He would never consider divorce and begged her forgiveness on his deathbed.

Mary of Modena (1658 – 1718), second wife of James II. Their marriage added to the downfall of James because his insistence on a Catholic bride enhanced the discontent of his subjects and caused the Glorious Revolution. When Mary of Modena gave birth to their son and heir James, the Protestants were compelled to act and invite William of Orange and his wife, James II's daughter Mary to take the throne. James II and his family fled to France and lived under the protection of the French King. The Protestants slandered young James by saying he was a changeling, spirited into the bed where Mary of Modena gave birth to him in a warming pan.

Mary II (1662 – 1694) was a light-hearted and pretty Stuart Princess, the eldest daughter of James II and Anne Hyde his first wife, when she was married to the much older and dour William of Orange. She went to her marriage bed soaked in tears but after many years Mary grew to esteem and adore her taciturn husband. When she was invited to rule England she insisted on a joint monarchy with him.

Anne (1665 – 1714), Queen Regnant, was the younger sister of Mary. She was ruled by favourites, principally by Sarah Churchill. Sarah was a strong, clever and ruthless woman who secured for herself and her husband titles and wealth. They became Duke and Duchess of Marlborough and through Anne they ruled the land. Anne and Sarah had no formality and called each other Mrs. Morley and Mrs. Freeman in private. Anne suffered greatly from the stillbirths and early deaths of all her nineteen pregnancies; only one son lived until he was eleven.

Sophia Dorothea of Celle (1666 – 1726) was the pretty wife and cousin of George Louis, Elector of Hanover, later George I of Great Britain, and mother of George II. Her marriage was one of political advantage and the couple despised each other. She was accused of an affair with Philip von Königsmarck that led to her being divorced and imprisoned in Castle of Ahlden for the last thirty years of her life. She was never officially queen of England but she was the mother of a King. Her son, George II, never forgave his father for treating his mother in this way.

Caroline of Brandenburg-Ansbach (1683 – 1737) was the wife of George II; she was plump, attractive and intellectual. She surrounded herself with cultured courtiers and politicians and ignored her husband's mistresses. She was the real power in the marriage and George listened to her. He mourned her death and never remarried.

Charlotte of Mecklenberg-Strelitz (1744 – 1818), queen of George III and mother of his fifteen children, thirteen of whom survived to adulthood. She loved music and was also an amateur botanist who helped expand Kew Gardens. She patiently cared for him during his mental breakdowns.

Caroline of Brunswick- Wolfenbüttel (1768 – 1821), the wife of the Prince Regent, George and later his queen when he became George IV. He was a famously fashionably dressed Prince and was probably already married to Maria Fitzherbert, a Catholic widow when he was forced to marry Caroline to try and cover his debts. She came from a small court and was very unfashionable and the Prince could not stand her on sight. Their child, Charlotte, died in childbirth and this caused a succession crisis because George III, despite having thirteen children had no legitimate grandchildren.

Adelaide of Saxe-Meiningen (1792 – 1849) was the Queen of William IV, who was the younger brother of George IV. When Princess Charlotte died William was one of the younger brothers who rushed to marry and attempt to have a child that would become the heir to the British throne. Adelaide had two stillbirths and no further children but she became very fond of the child who was born successfully to the Duke of Kent, Victoria.

Victoria (1819 – 1901), Queen Regnant of the United Kingdom and Ireland and Empress of India reigned for sixty-three years. She was an immensely popular figurehead. She was advised by a succession of prime ministers. She married Albert and had nine children. The marriage was very loving and she wore black for the rest of her life after his death.

Alexandra of Denmark (1844 – 1925) was the beautiful and popular Queen of Edward VII. She spent years as Princess of Wales and only nine years as Queen due to Victoria's longevity. She was a loving mother and was heartbroken when her eldest son Albert Victor died. Her sister Dagmar married the Russian Tsar and became Empress of Russia. During the revolution there was debate about offering sanctuary to the Russian royal family but George V thought it might incite violence and revolution in England.

Mary of Teck (1867 – 1953) was engaged to Albert Victor but upon his death married his younger brother the future King George V. Known as May by her family; Queen Mary was extremely dignified and renowned for keeping emotions private. Regal and formal, she was noted for her very extensive jewel collection. Her youngest son, John, had epilepsy and died aged thirteen.

Elizabeth Bowes Lyon (1900 – 2002) was born into a family of Scottish nobility and she married Albert, Duke of York; the second son of King George V. When Edward VIII abdicated 'Bertie' and Elizabeth became King George VI and she his queen. It was an unexpected role but they embraced it dutifully. They were very popular, especially as figureheads during the war.

Elizabeth II (born 1926) was expected to be a minor royal but upon her uncle's abdication became heir to the throne. Her father died young and she became Queen in 1952. She married Philip of Greece and has four children. Lines quoted are from former poet laureates Tennyson and Masefield.

This book could not have been written without my parents who encouraged me to be curious about everything and kept their house full of history books for me to read: thank you to Roger Gartland and Jayne Gartland.

Thanks to Julie MacLuskey.

Thanks to Tracey Hill; your seminars formed the backdrop of the Jacobean and Restoration poems in this collection.

I'm very grateful to the Arvon Foundation for a grant that meant I could spend a week at the Hurst, Shropshire working on the poems with advice from two excellent tutors: Fiona Sampson and David Harsent.

Thanks also to friends who gave me feedback; Adam Fuller, Katy Wareham Morris, Sarah James, Stephen Sanders and Jennifer Hope. Also appreciation goes to the wider group of poets, editors, event organisers and reviewers I have met over the last few years and who have encouraged my writing and published my poems.

Very special thanks to Fiona Sampson, David Arnold and Alison Weir for taking the time to read the manuscript and give me your endorsements.

'Anne Boleyn' is dedicated to Chloe Stopa-Hunt for reminding me of Iphigenia.

Thanks also to my editor Todd Swift for giving me the space to publish the queens at Eyewear and Edwin Smet for his design.

Finally: thank you to Lawrence, Pamela, Isaac and Theodore.

'Philippa of Hainault' uses the original description of her (or perhaps her sister) written by the Bishop Stapledon of Exeter, for the King.

'Isabella of Valois' uses lines from a traditional nursery rhyme.

'Katherine of Aragon' uses lines from her last letter to Henry VIII.

'Catharine Howard' uses lines from Thomas Wyatt's poem, 'And Wilt Thou Leave Me Thus?'

'Elizabeth I', the first two lines paraphrase a sermon by John Knox, and I use a line from one of her own verses, 'for I am soft and made of melting snow.'

'Jane Grey' uses lines from her letter to Mary I.

'Elizabeth Cromwell' paraphrases Luke 6:21 from The Holy Bible.

'Victoria' uses lines from her correspondence.

'Elizabeth II' lines quoted (as not her words) from Shakespeare and former poet laureates Tennyson and Masefield.

I would like to also thank Susan Howe. Her words perfectly encapsulate my intentions with this collection and are used as the preface to this work. The lines are from her prose piece; 'There Are Not Leaves Enough to Crown to Cover to Crown to Cover' – *The Europe of Trusts* (1990).

I would like to thank the following authors and historians for their invaluable books, which helped me so much in my research:

Alison Weir's *The Lady in the Tower; Isabella: She Wolf of France; Eleanor of Aquitaine: By the Wrath of God, Queen of England*; and *Elizabeth the Queen*.

Lisa Hilton's *Queens Consort: England's Medieval Queens*.

Elizabeth Norton's *She Wolves: The Notorious Queens of England*.

Antonia Fraser's *Cromwell: Our Chief of Men*; *Charles II*; *James IV & I*.

This is not a definitive list of all the books used to research this book, but these four authors particularly inspired me.

EYEWEAR PUBLISHING

EYEWEAR POETRY

MORGAN HARLOW MIDWEST RITUAL BURNING
KATE NOAKES CAPE TOWN
RICHARD LAMBERT NIGHT JOURNEY
SIMON JARVIS EIGHTEEN POEMS
ELSPETH SMITH DANGEROUS CAKES
CALEB KLACES BOTTLED AIR
GEORGE ELLIOTT CLARKE ILLICIT SONNETS
HANS VAN DE WAARSENBURG THE PAST IS NEVER DEAD
DAVID SHOOK OUR OBSIDIAN TONGUES
BARBARA MARSH TO THE BONEYARD
MARIELA GRIFFOR THE PSYCHIATRIST
DON SHARE UNION
SHEILA HILLIER HOTEL MOONMILK
FLOYD SKLOOT CLOSE READING
PENNY BOXALL SHIP OF THE LINE
MANDY KAHN MATH, HEAVEN, TIME
MARION MCCREADY TREE LANGUAGE
RUFO QUINTAVALLE WEATHER DERIVATIVES
SJ FOWLER THE ROTTWEILER'S GUIDE TO THE DOG OWNER
TEDI LÓPEZ MILLS DEATH ON RUA AUGUSTA
AGNIESZKA STUDZINSKA WHAT THINGS ARE
JEMMA BORG THE ILLUMINATED WORLD
KEIRAN GODDARD FOR THE CHORUS
COLETTE SENSIER SKINLESS
BENNO BARNARD A PUBLIC WOMAN
ANDREW SHIELDS THOMAS HARDY LISTENS TO LOUIS ARMSTRONG
JAN OWEN THE OFFHAND ANGEL
A.K. BLAKEMORE HUMBERT SUMMER
SEAN SINGER HONEY & SMOKE
RUTH STACEY QUEEN, JEWEL, MISTRESS

EYEWEAR PROSE

SUMIA SUKKAR THE BOY FROM ALEPPO WHO PAINTED THE WAR
ALFRED CORN MIRANDA'S BOOK

EYEWEAR LITERARY CRITICISM

MARK FORD THIS DIALOGUE OF ONE - WINNER OF THE 2015 PEGASUS AWARD
FOR POETRY CRITICISM FROM THE POETRY FOUNDATION (CHICAGO, USA).